I0902489

I'm praying you find comfort in the truth that nothing can stop God's plans for you.

"Whoever does the will of My Father in heaven is My brother and sister and mother."

MATTHEW 12:50

It's always possible to do the will of God, because God has given us the gifts that are essential to accomplish that job.

ELISABETH ELLIOT

DaySpring

For more inspiration, scan here:

I'm praying that God blesses you with His peace today.

"If God so clothes the grass of the field,
which today is, and tomorrow
is thrown into the oven,
will He not much more clothe you?"

MATTHEW 6:30

*In God's economy,
whether He is making a flower
or a human soul, nothing ever
comes to nothing. The losses
are His way of accomplishing gains.*

ELISABETH ELLIOT

DaySpring

For more inspiration, scan here:

I'm praying God gives you extra faith today.

Set your mind on things above,
not on things on the earth.
COLOSSIANS 3:2

I like to think of "faith" as a two-world word.
We are looking at the things
that are unseen while we're
doing the things that are seen.
The vision of the unseen will transform
the seen into something very glorious.
ELISABETH ELLIOT

DaySpring

For more inspiration, scan here:

I'm praying that you feel comforted and guided today.

Teach me to do Your will,
for You are my God.

PSALM 143:10

The very relinquishment of this thing that you so urgently desire is a true demonstration of the sincerity of your lifelong prayer: Thy will be done.

ELISABETH ELLIOT

DaySpring

For more inspiration, scan here:

Praying you feel God's love for you in the deepest, most truth-filled ways today.

The word of God is living and powerful, and sharper than any two-edged sword.

HEBREWS 4:12

How can God remold my mind from within unless I continually test what I read and hear from the world by the straightedge of Scripture?

ELISABETH ELLIOT

DaySpring

For more inspiration, scan here:

I'm praying you'll experience a sense of connectedness to God's big plan today.

For whom He foreknew,
He also predestined
to be conformed
to the image of His Son.

ROMANS 8:29

*Everything that happens
fits into a pattern for good,
but that pattern and that purpose
is to shape us to the likeness of His Son.*

ELISABETH ELLIOT

DaySpring

For more inspiration, scan here:

I'm praying for God's grace to cover over all your worries and cares today.

"Therefore do not worry about tomorrow, for tomorrow will worry about its own things. Sufficient for the day is its own trouble."

MATTHEW 6:34

Today's care, not tomorrow's, is the responsibility given to us, apportioned in the wisdom of God.

ELISABETH ELLIOT

DaySpring

For more inspiration, scan here:

Praying that God would give you the gift of contentment for all circumstances.

For I have learned
in whatever state I am,
to be content.
PHILIPPIANS 4:11

My prayer is: Teach me to receive thankfully those things in my life that cannot be changed.
ELISABETH ELLIOT

DaySpring

For more inspiration, scan here:

May you discover incredible, deep joy today, through whatever you are facing.

"These things I have spoken to you,
that My joy may remain in you,
and that your joy may be full."

JOHN 15:11

When we make our bodies a living sacrifice
to God—holy, acceptable unto Him—
what are we getting in return?
Eternal bliss, fulfillment, joy,
the expulsive power of a new affection.

ELISABETH ELLIOT

For more inspiration, scan here:

Praying for peace for your heart and mind today.

Christ Jesus . . . humbled Himself
and became obedient to the point of death,
even the death of the cross.

PHILIPPIANS 2:5, 8

Almighty God humbled Himself, coming into the world like every other baby— through a mother's womb. Think of the humility! He was saying, "Everything is the reverse of what it appears. But don't be afraid. I know what I'm doing."

ELISABETH ELLIOT

For more
inspiration,
scan here:

May God bless you with calm, peace, hope, and joy today.

The Lamb will overcome them,
for He is Lord of lords and King of kings;
and those who are with Him are called,
chosen, and faithful.

REVELATION 17:14

There is nothing on earth or in hell or in heaven, in time or in eternity, that can alter in any final sense what God has promised—because all things serve Him.

ELISABETH ELLIOT

DaySpring

For more inspiration, scan here:

I'm asking God to fill you with His peace today.

The peace of God, which surpasses all understanding, will guard your hearts and minds through Christ Jesus.

PHILIPPIANS 4:7

The peace of God means the absence of conflict with the will of God. It means harmony within, concord with His purpose for our lives.

ELISABETH ELLIOT

For more inspiration, scan here:

I'm praying as you seek God's direction today.

He who searches the hearts
knows what the mind of the Spirit is,
because He makes intercession for the saints
according to the will of God.

ROMANS 8:27

Prayer is not so much the means
whereby God's will is bent to our desires
as it is whereby our desires are bent to God's will.

ELISABETH ELLIOT

DaySpring

For more
inspiration,
scan here:

I'm praying that your heart absolutely delights in God and His gifts for you today.

Delight yourself also in the LORD,
and He shall give you the desires of your heart.

PSALM 37:4

Lord, may no gift of Yours ever take Your place in my heart. Help me to hold Your gifts lightly in an open palm, that the supreme object of my desire may always be You and You alone.

ELISABETH ELLIOT

For more inspiration, scan here:

I'm asking God to closely lead you in your decisions and thoughts today.

For the kingdom of God is not eating and drinking, but righteousness and peace and joy in the Holy Spirit.

ROMANS 14:17

If you seek first the kingdom of God, it will be impossible to miss not just happiness but also the deepest joy.

ELISABETH ELLIOT

DaySpring

For more inspiration, scan here:

May His presence and love feel so close to you as you wait.

My soul, wait silently for God alone,
for my expectation is from Him.

PSALM 62:5

Nothing can be more spiritually nourishing than waiting on God. He keeps me waiting, sometimes to what looks to me like the "screaming edge" of the precipice. Then precisely when I need to know, God shows me.

ELISABETH ELLIOT

DaySpring

For more inspiration, scan here:

I'm praying for God's wisdom in all your experiences today!

*I have rejoiced in the way
of Your testimonies,
as much as in all riches.*

PSALM 119:14

If we aim at happiness in this world,
we will probably miss the mark of holiness.
But if we aim at holiness, we can't fail to be happy.

ELISABETH ELLIOT

DaySpring

For more inspiration, scan here:

Thanking God today for His perfect plan for your life.

"For I know the plans I have for you,"
declares the LORD,
"plans to prosper you
and not to harm you,
plans to give you hope and a future."

JEREMIAH 29:11 NIV

God knows what is good for each of us, and He puts us in the place of His choice.

ELISABETH ELLIOT

DaySpring

For more
inspiration,
scan here:

You have a tough decision ahead, but God will lead you through. I'm praying for you.

He who says he abides in Him
ought himself also to walk just as He walked.

I JOHN 2:6

The knowledge of God is not an intellectual exercise.
It is the reward of loving obedience.
Obedience is the only valid proof of our love for Him.

ELISABETH ELLIOT

DaySpring

For more
inspiration,
scan here:

Asking God to give you extra endurance and strength today.

Let us run with endurance the race
that is set before us, looking unto Jesus,
the author and finisher of our faith.

HEBREWS 12:1-2

The best means to spiritual equilibrium
is to look repeatedly at the things
that are not seen, that is,
at things that are eternal.

ELISABETH ELLIOT

DaySpring

For more inspiration, scan here:

May God's nearness and tender care fill you with peace today.

The Lord searches all hearts and understands all the intent of the thoughts.

I CHRONICLES 28:9

You have no secrets that God does not know.

ELISABETH ELLIOT

For more
inspiration,
scan here:

Asking God to reassure you that you have all you need for this moment.

"Be not dismayed, for I am your God.
I will strengthen you, yes, I will help you,
I will uphold you with My righteous right hand."

ISAIAH 41:10

God never asks us to do anything for which He does not supply the time, the strength, and the gifts.

ELISABETH ELLIOT

DaySpring

For more inspiration, scan here:

Praying that you would feel the uplifting and strengthening arms of God today.

Do not grow weary in doing good.

II THESSALONIANS 3:13

God wants perseverance.
He wants faithfulness, loyalty, and the willingness
to stick with the job that He has given us.

ELISABETH ELLIOT

DaySpring

For more inspiration, scan here:

May your trust in Him be rewarded with peace, joy, and deep gratitude.

In God we boast all day long,
and praise Your name forever.

PSALM 44:8

The true Christian is thankful for all things. How is it possible to be thankful for all things? Because we trust Him. Trust is the ground of our thanksgiving.

ELISABETH ELLIOT

For more inspiration, scan here:

Asking God to remind you of His incredible love toward you.

*I will worship toward Your holy temple,
and praise Your name for Your lovingkindness
and Your truth; for You have magnified
Your word above all Your name.*

PSALM 138:2

There is always plenty to complain about if your life is controlled by your feelings. But there is always much more to thank God for if your life is controlled by your dwelling on His faithfulness, His love, and His mercy.

ELISABETH ELLIOT

DaySpring

For more
inspiration,
scan here:

May the hope of Jesus envelop and overwhelm you today.

But if we hope for what we do not see, we eagerly wait for it with perseverance.

ROMANS 8:25

Even when something heartwrenchingly tragic happens, hope keeps us going. For we know that we are loved with an everlasting love. One day we will see that our hope was not in vain.

ELISABETH ELLIOT

DaySpring

For more inspiration, scan here:

Today, may God remind you of your strengths and meet you in your limitations.

I will run the course of
Your commandments,
for You shall enlarge my heart.
PSALM 119:32

The course God sets for us in His commandments is not an obstacle course but one carefully planned to suit our qualifications—not too rigorous for our limitations, not too lenient for our strengths.
ELISABETH ELLIOT

DaySpring

For more inspiration, scan here:

Asking God to make His voice and purpose for you very clear.

"Be still, and know that I am God."

PSALM 46:10

Have we learned to stand in silence with our mouths shut and our hearts open? We must be quiet in order to know Him.

ELISABETH ELLIOT

DaySpring

For more
inspiration,
scan here:

May your reasons to be thankful be obvious and plenty today.

Strengthened with all might, according to His glorious power . . . [give] thanks to the Father.

COLOSSIANS 1:11-12

It takes power to thank the Father when everything in us protests. But we find in Him (not always in what happens to us) plenty of reason to thank Him and plenty of power.

ELISABETH ELLIOT

DaySpring

For more
inspiration,
scan here:

Praying you may experience God's precious generosity today!

What You give them they gather in;
You open Your hand,
they are filled with good.
PSALM 104:28

There is no such thing as something "too good to be true." God is loving and lavishly generous and has promised to give what is good—that is, what He who is omniscient knows to be good for us.

ELISABETH ELLIOT

DaySpring

For more inspiration, scan here:

I'm praying that you feel strengthened and able in the coming days.

Every good gift and every perfect gift is from above, and comes down from the Father of lights.

JAMES 1:17

As God apportions the work, the burdens, the surprises, the interruptions, He never forgets to apportion also the strength and the grace that we will need.

ELISABETH ELLIOT

DaySpring

For more inspiration, scan here:

Praying that God's love would both fuel and inspire you today.

Many waters cannot quench love,
nor can the floods drown it.

SONG OF SOLOMON 8:7

*Love leads us where we did not intend to go,
where we would not have chosen to go
if we had known the whole story
ahead of time.*

ELISABETH ELLIOT

DaySpring

For more
inspiration,
scan here:

I'm asking God to bless and fulfill you today.

Our help is in the name of the L*ORD*,
who made heaven and earth.

PSALM 124:8

The more hopeless and helpless we feel,
the more we must believe that there is someone
far greater than us, someone who loves us,
who wants to take over our lives—
for our blessing and our fulfillment.

ELISABETH ELLIOT

DaySpring

For more inspiration, scan here:

I'm praying your faith continues to grow—not just in words but in the way you live and love.

That you may walk worthy of the Lord, fully pleasing Him, being fruitful in every good work and increasing in the knowledge of God.

COLOSSIANS 1:10

True faith is action. Faith comes by hearing and results in doing.

ELISABETH ELLIOT

For more inspiration, scan here:

Asking God to fill you with His peaceful presence today.

"These things I have spoken to you, that in Me you may have peace."

JOHN 16:33

Only with a robust faith and active prayer life can you live in peace in the tensions of this world.

ELISABETH ELLIOT

DaySpring

For more
inspiration,
scan here:

I'm praying for you today— for your enjoyment and delight at whatever comes your way.

"If you . . . know how to give good gifts to your children, how much more will your Father who is in heaven give good things to those who ask Him!"

MATTHEW 7:11

The Lord gives us daily, not weekly, bread. He gives strength according to our days, not our years. The work, the suffering, the joy are given according to His careful measure.

ELISABETH ELLIOT

DaySpring

For more inspiration, scan here:

Praying over your connections today, that you're blessed as you bless others.

Let us consider one another in order to stir up love and good works.

HEBREWS 10:24

There may be somebody who needs you today. If you're in communion with the same Father with whom Jesus was in communion, you can respond to that person's need.

ELISABETH ELLIOT

For more inspiration, scan here:

May you see things God's way today and get excited!

"For with God
all things are possible."

MARK 10:27

A renewed mind has an utterly changed conception, not only of reality but of possibility. Impossibilities become possibilities.

ELISABETH ELLIOT

DaySpring

For more inspiration, scan here:

You're on my heart today, and I'm praying for you.

But grow in the grace
and knowledge of
our Lord and Savior Jesus Christ.

II PETER 3:18

Are you troubled about something
that looms ahead?
God will give you the next grace
for the next thing you need to do.
It will always be enough.

ELISABETH ELLIOT

DaySpring

For more
inspiration,
scan here:

Praying that today God's good gifts would overwhelm you with love.

He who did not spare His own Son,
but delivered Him up for us all,
how shall He not with Him
also freely give us all things?

ROMANS 8:32

It is God's nature to give. He can no more "help" giving than He can "help" loving. He will give us everything in the world that is good for us.

ELISABETH ELLIOT

DaySpring

For more
inspiration,
scan here:

I'm asking God to refresh your spirit and bring you joy today.

If you extend your soul to the hungry and satisfy the afflicted soul . . . you shall be like a watered garden, and like a spring of water, whose waters do not fail.

ISAIAH 58:10-11

When I am in need of refreshment, I have found that if, instead of praying for my own comfort and satisfaction, I ask the Lord to enable me to give to others, an amazing thing often happens—I find my own needs wonderfully met.

ELISABETH ELLIOT

DaySpring

For more inspiration, scan here:

May thankfulness overtake your thoughts today. I'm praying!

Oh, give thanks to the LORD,
for He is good!
For His mercy endures forever.

PSALM 118:1

When you face what can't be solved immediately and you don't know how you are going to get through the next day or the next week, try thanking God in advance for His help. He is our helper.

ELISABETH ELLIOT

DaySpring

For more
inspiration,
scan here:

Asking God to guide your steps today.

A man's heart plans his way,
but the LORD directs his steps.

PROVERBS 16:9

God doesn't do anything without a purpose.
God has created us with a purpose
to fulfill and a place to be.
He has given us each a job
that nobody else can do.

ELISABETH ELLIOT

DaySpring

For more inspiration, scan here:

I'm praying you find rest. God is working, even when it doesn't feel like it.

All things work together for good to those who love God, to those who are the called according to His purpose.

ROMANS 8:28

Faith already knows that everything that happens fits into a pattern for good to those who love God. An inconvenience is always, whether we see it or not, a blessed inconvenience.

ELISABETH ELLIOT

DaySpring

For more
inspiration,
scan here:

Asking God to fill you with His peace today.

And let the peace of God rule in your hearts, to which also you were called in one body; and be thankful.

COLOSSIANS 3:15

God's will is our peace. The sooner we learn
to love Him and to love His will
and to surrender ourselves wholeheartedly
and gladly into those everlasting arms,
the sooner we will find our peace.

ELISABETH ELLIOT

For more
inspiration,
scan here:

I'm praying that God's goodness and greatness will be your hope and strength today.

"I am God, and there is none like Me."

ISAIAH 46:9

We cannot control events, but we can control how we respond to them. When things happen that dismay or appall, we ought to remember that God is not taken by surprise nor can His purposes be thwarted in the end.

ELISABETH ELLIOT

DaySpring

For more inspiration, scan here:

May God grant you understanding as you continue on the path that He has prepared for you.

By awesome deeds in righteousness You will answer us, O God of our salvation.

PSALM 65:5

God has a good many reasons for saying no to our prayers, and I'm learning as I grow older that many of God's greatest mercies are His refusals.

ELISABETH ELLIOT

DaySpring

For more inspiration, scan here:

Asking God to help you order your days in peaceful ways.

But as for me, I trust in You, O LORD;
I say, "You are my God."
My times are in Your hand.

PSALM 31:14-15

You have exactly what God has measured out as being sufficient in time. There is always time to get done what He wants you to do. Pray that He will make you a faithful steward of the time He gives you.

ELISABETH ELLIOT

For more
inspiration,
scan here:

I'm praying that God would steady your heart and guide your steps today.

You will keep him in perfect peace,
whose mind is stayed on You,
because he trusts in You.

ISAIAH 26:3

Speak that word to me today, dear Lord: peace.
Let your calm spirit—through the
many potentially rough minutes of this day,
in every task—say to my soul, "Be still."

ELISABETH ELLIOT

DaySpring

For more
inspiration,
scan here:

I'm praying, as you are praying, that God would encourage your heart.

Pray without ceasing.

I THESSALONIANS 5:17

Don't ever imagine that anything is too small to pray about. If it concerns you, it concerns God.

ELISABETH ELLIOT

DaySpring

For more inspiration, scan here:

Praying and trusting that God is holding you close today.

You established the earth, and it abides. They continue this day according to Your ordinances, for all are Your servants.

PSALM 119:90-91

He manages perfectly, day and night, year in and year out, the movements of the stars, the wheeling of the planets, the staggering coordination of events. There is no doubt that He can manage the timing of my days and weeks.

ELISABETH ELLIOT

DaySpring

For more inspiration, scan here:

May God give you so many reasons to smile and give thanks today.

In everything give thanks;
for this is the will of God
in Christ Jesus for you.

I THESSALONIANS 5:18

Gratitude springs from acceptance of the gifts, the conditions and circumstances that God gives us.

ELISABETH ELLIOT

For more
inspiration,
scan here:

Asking God to strengthen you with His comfort and peace today.

Blessed be the God and Father
of our Lord Jesus Christ . . .
who comforts us in all our tribulation.

II CORINTHIANS 1:3-4

A life free from suffering would be a life
in which faith in God would be a mere frill.
A human life, on the contrary,
is one in which faith is a necessity.

ELISABETH ELLIOT

DaySpring

For more
inspiration,
scan here:

I'm praying that you get a strong sense of how much you matter—because you really do.

As each one has received a gift,
minister it to one another,
as good stewards of
the manifold grace of God.

I PETER 4:10

Maybe you haven't been able to discern any specific gift that God has given to you, but I believe that eternity may show that you yourself have been a gift to somebody.

ELISABETH ELLIOT

DaySpring

For more inspiration, scan here:

I'm praying for you, friend. Hang in there and keep trusting.

And the Lord will deliver me
from every evil work
and preserve me for His heavenly kingdom.

II TIMOTHY 4:18

Maybe you see no way out of your situation,
no light at the end of the tunnel.
In God's time He will deliver you. He is your strength.

ELISABETH ELLIOT

DaySpring

For more
inspiration,
scan here:

Today I'm thanking God for you. Your servant's heart is a blessing.

"He who is faithful
in what is least is faithful also in much."

LUKE 16:10

We are called to be exceptional
in the ordinary things,
faithful in the little things,
trustworthy when nobody's looking.

ELISABETH ELLIOT

DaySpring

For more
inspiration,
scan here:

As you're waiting, know that I'm praying for you.

See how the farmer waits
for the precious fruit of the earth,
waiting patiently for it until
it receives the early and latter rain.
You also be patient.

JAMES 5:7-8

If we could simply remember that this is true of everything—that God's purposes are slowly being worked out for His glory and our good—we would, like the farmer, keep faith and wait quietly.

ELISABETH ELLIOT

For more
inspiration,
scan here:

Asking God to give you His comfort and reassuring love today.

To everything there is a season,
a time for every purpose under heaven.

ECCLESIASTES 3:1

In God's economy, whether He is
making a flower or a human soul,
nothing ever comes to nothing.
The losses are His way of accomplishing the gains.

ELISABETH ELLIOT

DaySpring

For more inspiration, scan here:

May your load be light and God's peace ever present. I'm praying!

"My yoke is easy and My burden is light."

MATTHEW 11:30

We need to learn to walk side by side with Him, bearing humbly and gently the yoke He places on us. If we do this, any burden He allows—of loss or pain or insult or responsibility or heartbreak—will be both bearable and light.

ELISABETH ELLIOT

DaySpring

For more
inspiration,
scan here:

Praying for your today and tomorrow, knowing that God will be faithful to lead you through.

You do not know what will
happen tomorrow . . .
You ought to say,
"If the Lord wills,
we shall live and do this or that."

JAMES 4:14-15

God is always in the business of preparing us and shaping us for whatever tomorrow may bring forth.

ELISABETH ELLIOT

DaySpring

For more inspiration, scan here:

I'm praying that you may see God's goodness as He continues to write your story.

But I want you to know . . . that the things which happened to me have actually turned out for the furtherance of the gospel.

PHILIPPIANS 1:12

Put each difficult thing in your hands and offer it up to Jesus. You might be amazed at how God can transform that thing that is so painful to you into good for somebody else.

ELISABETH ELLIOT

DaySpring

For more inspiration, scan here:

I'm praying with my whole heart for everything you need today.

Whatever we ask we receive from Him, because we keep His commandments and do those things that are pleasing in His sight.

I JOHN 3:22

When our prayers are exactly in accord with what our Heavenly Father has in mind, we can be assured that the answer will be yes.

ELISABETH ELLIOT

DaySpring

For more inspiration, scan here:

Asking God to bless your waiting with wisdom, patience, and peace.

The Lord is good to those who wait for Him, to the soul who seeks Him.

LAMENTATIONS 3:25

When I want what God knows I'm not ready for, I must be willing to wait.

ELISABETH ELLIOT

DaySpring

For more inspiration, scan here:

I'm praying you feel the courage and strength you need for whatever lies ahead.

I can do all things through Christ who strengthens me.

PHILIPPIANS 4:13

God sometimes asks of us things that look impossible, but they never turn out to be—because God's command is always His enabling.

ELISABETH ELLIOT

DaySpring

For more inspiration, scan here:

May God's power, love, and presence guide your every thought today.

For God has not given us
a spirit of fear, but of power
and of love and of a sound mind.

II TIMOTHY 1:7

Nobody ever failed to do the will of God because he was too weak, too poor, too old, too ignorant, or didn't have time. God has promised that He will give you the strength, the knowledge, and the time to do whatever He wants you to do.

ELISABETH ELLIOT

For more inspiration, scan here:

Asking God to make your special gifts known to you in ways that make you feel valued, seen, and loved.

There are diversities of gifts . . .
but one and the same Spirit works
all these things, distributing to
each one individually as He wills.

I CORINTHIANS 12:4, 11

*My limitations become,
in the sovereignty of God, gifts.
For it is with the equipment that I
have been given that I am to glorify God.*

ELISABETH ELLIOT

DaySpring

For more inspiration, scan here:

I'm praying today that you see God's goodness at every turn.

The kingdoms of this world have become the kingdoms of our Lord and of His Christ.

REVELATION 11:15

God is sovereign and knows how to turn the evil of the world into the blessings of His kingdom.

ELISABETH ELLIOT

DaySpring

For more
inspiration,
scan here:

May God's strength be your strength today.

For when I am weak,
then I am strong.
II CORINTHIANS 12:10

On those days when you feel you have not enough strength for your own tasks, you might be amazed to discover that God can supply strength even to give away.

ELISABETH ELLIOT

DaySpring

For more
inspiration,
scan here:

I'm thanking God for you today and asking Him to encourage you with His love and grace.

Be kindly affectionate
to one another with brotherly love.

ROMANS 12:10

Perhaps one of the most neglected graces in the world is the simple, honest ability to tell people that we appreciate them.

ELISABETH ELLIOT

DaySpring

For more
inspiration,
scan here:

Asking our generous God to bless your steps today.

He gives power to the weak, and to those who have no might He increases strength.

ISAIAH 40:29

The Lord, the everlasting God, creator of the wide world, grows neither weary nor faint; and yet He's ready to give vigor to those of us who are weary.

ELISABETH ELLIOT

For more inspiration, scan here:

I'm praying for you as you trust in God for big things.

God is our refuge and strength,
a very present help in trouble.

PSALM 46:1

If we were never afraid, how could we know God as a refuge and fortress? It is our very weakness that gives us occasion to call on Him.

ELISABETH ELLIOT

DaySpring

For more inspiration, scan here:

May God's faithfulness be your comfort today. I'm praying for you!

My help comes from the LORD,
who made heaven and earth.

PSALM 121:2

*Lord, I believe. Help my unbelief.
Give me a trust big enough to embrace
the baffling intricacies and to find
in times of helplessness
that You are a very present help.*

ELISABETH ELLIOT

DaySpring

For more
inspiration,
scan here:

I'm praying you feel the encouragement and love that others feel from you so often.

For God is not unjust to forget your work and labor of love which you have shown toward His name, in that you have ministered to the saints, and do minister.

HEBREWS 6:10

If with courage and joy we pour ourselves out for Him and for others for His sake, it is not possible to lose, in any final sense, anything worth keeping.

ELISABETH ELLIOT

DaySpring

For more
inspiration,
scan here:

Asking God to give you the confidence you need to move forward in joy today.

"I am the good shepherd; and I know My sheep, and am known by My own."

JOHN 10:14

It is not for the flock of sheep to know the pasture the Shepherd has in mind. It is for them simply to follow Him.

ELISABETH ELLIOT

For more
inspiration,
scan here:

I'm trusting God to love you well as you wait on His perfect timing.

Those who wait on the LORD shall renew their strength.

ISAIAH 40:31

I think perhaps the hardest lesson of faith is learning to wait. We always want to do something, and sometimes God says, "Don't do anything. Be still. Listen to Me."

ELISABETH ELLIOT

DaySpring

For more inspiration, scan here:

Thanking God and praying for you as you prayerfully do His work today.

For we are God's masterpiece. He has created us anew in Christ Jesus, so we can do the good things He planned for us long ago.

EPHESIANS 2:10 NLT

Prayer is very hard work, but I'm convinced that it's the most important work that we can do for God.

ELISABETH ELLIOT

DaySpring

For more inspiration, scan here:

I see you, and I'm praying for you today.

I am already being poured out as a drink offering.

II TIMOTHY 4:6

We should be willing to be used and to be used up, according to the will of God.

ELISABETH ELLIOT

For more
inspiration,
scan here:

Asking God to make sure you get all the love and encouragement you need today.

"He who loves Me will be
loved by My Father,
and I will love him
and manifest Myself to him."

JOHN 14:21

It's hard to give out love and encouragement when you yourself don't feel loved and encouraged. That is why you need to go to God daily for love and support. His care for you makes it possible for you to care for others.

ELISABETH ELLIOT

DaySpring

For more
inspiration,
scan here:

May God's strength and empathy lift your spirits and lead you forward today.

For we do not have a High Priest who cannot sympathize with our weaknesses, but was in all points tempted as we are, yet without sin.

HEBREWS 4:15

When you are tempted, remember that Jesus understands the wilderness in which you find yourself. You aren't alone. He is touched with the feeling of your infirmity, and He is ready to help.

ELISABETH ELLIOT

For more inspiration, scan here:

Praying that God would encourage your heart with just the right message today.

"The grass withers, the flower fades, but the word of our God stands forever."

ISAIAH 40:8

The Bible is my anchor.
It holds me in the storms of life.
It is the one thing that is constant
in all the swaying to and fro
of the opinions and fashions
of modern thinking.

ELISABETH ELLIOT

For more inspiration, scan here:

I'm praying for you in this season, friend. You're stronger than you think.

Many are the afflictions
of the righteous, but the LORD
delivers him out of them all.

PSALM 34:19

To me it makes a tremendous difference to know that nothing is for nothing.
God always has a purpose for us.

ELISABETH ELLIOT

DaySpring

For more
inspiration,
scan here:

Asking God to give you His comfort and joy today.

I am filled with comfort.
I am exceedingly joyful in all our tribulation.

II CORINTHIANS 7:4

Anything worth having is worth waiting for. Troubles are permitted in order to teach us many lessons, not the least of which is patience.

ELISABETH ELLIOT

DaySpring

For more inspiration, scan here:

Asking God to lead you lovingly in all the details of your ordinary day.

Take careful heed . . .
to love the LORD your God,
to walk in all His ways,
to keep His commandments.

JOSHUA 22:5

It is the desire of my heart to love God. And there is no other place where I can learn to do this except in my ordinary, everyday life.

ELISABETH ELLIOT

For more
inspiration,
scan here:

I'm praying you would feel God's closeness to you at every step along the journey.

"I will never leave you nor forsake you."

HEBREWS 13:5

He cannot and will not forsake us, who are not only His sons and daughters but also the dwelling-places of His only begotten Son.

ELISABETH ELLIOT

DaySpring

For more inspiration, scan here:

May you know the power of prayer and the gift of thanksgiving in all your ways today.

Continue earnestly in prayer,
being vigilant in it with thanksgiving.

COLOSSIANS 4:2

If God is sovereign and things will be as they are going to be anyway, why bother to pray? God has told us to pray. It is a commandment, and if we love Him, we obey His commands.

ELISABETH ELLIOT

DaySpring

For more
inspiration,
scan here:

You've got this,
and God has you.
I'm praying
for you today!

Be strong in the grace
that is in Christ Jesus.

II TIMOTHY 2:1

Where shall I ever find the strength
I need to get through this experience,
this ordeal, this day, this week?
The answer is: Take it!
Take it from the grace that is ours
already in Christ Jesus.

ELISABETH ELLIOT

DaySpring

For more inspiration, scan here:

I'm praying that you recognize the incredible gifts of God all over your life today.

Blessed be the Lord, who daily loads us with benefits, the God of our salvation!

PSALM 68:19

When God gives you a gift, you can be sure that even if it was not what you had in mind, it is even better for you; because He knows exactly the things that are appropriate to the job He wants you to do.

ELISABETH ELLIOT

DaySpring

For more inspiration, scan here:

Praying that today you feel confident that your efforts are making a difference.

So whether you eat or drink
or whatever you do,
do it all for the glory of God.

I CORINTHIANS 10:31 NIV

Whatever you are doing,
put your whole heart into it,
as if you were doing it
for the Lord and not for men.

ELISABETH ELLIOT

DaySpring

For more inspiration, scan here:

Asking God to encourage your heart today.

*The humble He guides in justice,
and the humble He teaches His way.*

PSALM 25:9

If you're looking for God's guidance
and God doesn't seem to be in a hurry
to give it to you, plod faithfully along,
doing what you know He wants you to do.

ELISABETH ELLIOT

DaySpring

For more inspiration, scan here:

I'm praying for you today as you step faithfully forward.

To be spiritually minded
is life and peace.

ROMANS 8:6

In God's will is my peace,
which is infinitely,
immeasurably, and unspeakably
beyond imagination.

ELISABETH ELLIOT

For more inspiration, scan here:

Asking God not to hold back on the joy He brings you today.

Now may the God of hope
fill you with all joy
and peace in believing.

ROMANS 15:13

I am absolutely convinced that God, because He is a loving Father, cannot possibly want for us anything less than joy.

ELISABETH ELLIOT

DaySpring

For more inspiration, scan here:

I'm praying that you find delight in all the good ways that God is at work in your life.

For all things are for your sakes, that grace, having spread through the many, may cause thanksgiving to abound to the glory of God.

II CORINTHIANS 4:15

The mystery of God's sovereignty
is that His everlasting love
is being worked out in all the happenings
of history—for His glory and our joy.

ELISABETH ELLIOT

DaySpring

For more
inspiration,
scan here:

Today I'm lifting you up with faith that God has so much good for you ahead.

"I have come that they may have life, and that they may have it more abundantly."

JOHN 10:10

The message of the cross is transformation.
We bring our sufferings, and Christ gives us joy.
We bring our pains, and He gives us comfort.
We bring our deaths, and He gives us life.

ELISABETH ELLIOT

DaySpring

For more
inspiration,
scan here:

As you continue to trust God and pray, know that I'm praying right alongside you.

Evening and morning and at noon I will pray,
and cry aloud, and He shall hear my voice.

PSALM 55:17

Prayer is like breathing.
It is the air in which we survive spiritually.

ELISABETH ELLIOT

DaySpring

For more
inspiration,
scan here:

I'm praying for you, friend, and thanking God for the good work He's doing in your life.

That I may know Him and the power of His resurrection, and the fellowship of His sufferings, being conformed to His death.

PHILIPPIANS 3:10

To know Christ is to be made like Him. It is in beholding the image that we are changed into it, transformed by what we love.

ELISABETH ELLIOT

DaySpring

For more inspiration, scan here:

Asking God to make His love known to you in big ways today.

In this the love of God was manifested
toward us, that God has
sent His only begotten Son into the world,
that we might live through Him.

I JOHN 4:9

The Love that calls us into being,
woos us to Himself, makes us His bride,
lays down His life for us,
daily crowns us with lovingkindness
and tender mercy, will never abandon us.

ELISABETH ELLIOT

DaySpring

For more inspiration, scan here:

May the God of hope inundate you with it today. I'm praying for you!

This hope we have as an anchor of the soul, both sure and steadfast, and which enters the Presence behind the veil, where the forerunner has entered for us, even Jesus.

HEBREWS 6:19-20

The hope we have is a living hope. We wait for it, in faith and patience. Christ is the resurrection and the life. No wonder Easter is the greatest of Christian feast days! No wonder Christians sing!

ELISABETH ELLIOT

For more inspiration, scan here:

Lifting you up in prayer as you step forward today with courage.

The LORD is my light and my salvation;
whom shall I fear?

PSALM 27:1

*To fear God—that is,
to reverence and worship Him
in absolute assurance
of His sovereignty—
is to fear nothing else.*

ELISABETH ELLIOT

For more
inspiration,
scan here:

Praying you experience the deep love and value that God has for you, His precious child.

And whatever you do, do it heartily, as to the Lord and not to men, knowing that from the Lord you will receive the reward of the inheritance; for you serve the Lord Christ.

COLOSSIANS 3:23-24

The fine thing is for God so to occupy our thoughts that it is really nothing to us whether others treat us well or ill.

ELISABETH ELLIOT

DaySpring

For more inspiration, scan here:

I'm praying for you, that you would experience the full depth of God's love and fulfillment.

"The water that I shall give him
will become in him a fountain of water
springing up into everlasting life."

JOHN 4:14

It is my desire and aim to learn the beauty of Christ and to drink the Water of Life to the point where I am fully satisfied.

ELISABETH ELLIOT

DaySpring

For more
inspiration,
scan here: